Understanding 2 Thessalonians

Using Semitic Bible Study Methods with a new foundation

Michael Harvey Koplitz & Sandra Jean Koplitz

The NASB uses italic to show words that have been added for clarification. Citations are shown with large capital letters.

Published by Michael H. Koplitz

Table of Contents

Introduction..5

Culture and Language...9

The Aramaic Version of the New Testament...............................13

The Messianic Tradition Change...15

The Kabbalah..17

Methodology...19

Introduction to the Letter..25

Chapter One...27

Chapter Two...43

Chapter Three...57

Bibliography..69

Introduction

When a person is baptized as an infant and grows up in the church, different paradigms become a part of their religious DNA. The church has a message to give about Jesus Christ and His importance. Very few people study the theology and doctrines of the church to determine for themselves the accuracy of the church. The Proto-Orthodox church, which survived the pressures of the Roman Empire, decided in its infancy to oppose any expression of Christianity that did not fit its dogma. In addition, the Proto-Orthodox church would permanently destroy any writings that the rival Christians had developed.

The Gnostic Christians of Northern Egypt viewed the life of Jesus of Nazareth in a completely different way than the Proto-Orthodox church did. They saw the message about the Kingdom of Heaven as the vital purpose of Jesus. His birth, death, and Resurrection are not mentioned in the Gnostic Gospels. However, did the Proto-Orthodox church destroy the Gnostic Gospels when they crushed said movement? The answer is yes and no. Yes, they destroyed what they got their hands on. No, because in 1948, copies of the Gnostic religious books were discovered in Alexandria, Egypt. Once these documents were translated, the world learned what the Gnostic Christians believed. It is fascinatingly different than what the Proto-Orthodox said about these followers of Christ.

Why is this understanding critical? Much research points to a different situation in the early years than what the church espouses. A lot of this information is available to anyone today. However, the Seminaries and churches will not openly talk about these other writings about Jesus and His disciples. The scholars teaching in most Seminaries have learned their lessons from the church and from closed-minded mentors who refuse to look at other possibilities. This is because the Western European world took Christianity and changed it from a Near Eastern religion to a Western religion.

There is a theory that Paul converted Mithras House Churches into Jesus House Churches. This is clear from the connection between the Mithras' and Christianity's rituals. For example, baptism was the initiation ritual of Mithras. Communion did not originate with Jesus. This ritual was a part of Mithras where the followers would share his flesh (bread) and drink his blood (wine). There are many more rituals that Christianity picked up from Mithras. A good reference is "Christianity's Need for Mithras," which the author wrote.

Did Paul create the churches in the letters he sent, which comprise the New Testament, and if so, they must have been Jewish groups who became Jewish-Christians? They would have continued with their Hebraic rituals and saw Jesus of Nazareth as the Messiah that the prophets of old had promised. They would have adopted as many as Jesus' teachings and tried to live by them. The letters in the New Testament are written in Greek. However, most Jews in the Roman Empire did not speak Greek; instead, they spoke Aramaic and Hebrew. These congregations would not have understood a Greek letter from Paul.

Therefore, the letters in the New Testament must have been written in Aramaic and then transliterated into Greek. The same can be said for the Gospels, all of them. The church, over the centuries, decided who wrote the Gospels and what their intent was. The only Gospel we can assign to a writer is Luke. The other three are up in the air about who actually wrote them. While in Seminary, the author was taught that the entire New Testament was originally written in Koine Greek. However, that raised the question of, "Did Jesus speak Greek?" The Seminary instructors said, "no, Jesus did not speak Greek." Then the New Testament, especially the Gospels, must have been written in Aramaic. After all, Jesus spoke Aramaic and Hebrew.

We know this because He was a poor *tekton* (a stonemason or carpenter) from an impoverished city named Nazareth. Being born to a Jewish family in Galilee, he would have learned the traditions of His people and trade. He would have learned to speak Aramaic, the language of the area. He would have learned Hebrew because that was the language of the synagogue and the Temple in Jerusalem. In other words, Hebrew was the language of God, and Jewish males learned the language.

Suppose you are ready to toss this manuscript into the nearest trash can or delete it off your electronic device at this point in the introduction. In that case, the writer has your attention. This is the reaction when the writer has spoken with persons who had been indoctrinated into the church's position since birth. The author did not come into the church environment until he was 35. Therefore, the church's paradigms, dogma, and doctrine were not a part of his DNA. Instead, he questioned a lot. He found many inconsistencies between the Bible and the doctrines of the church. Seminary was an experience to learn what the church had evolved into two-thousand years after the death of Jesus.

There are more parts to the overall premise that the New Testament was originally written in Aramaic and will be explored. For the reader to grasp the subsequent phases of the proof, an open mind is critical.

Culture and Language

Let us continue in the journey of examining the New Testament to determine its original language. Nothing in stone tells us that Aramaic is the Original Language of the New Testament. However, nothing says that Koine Greek was the original language of the New Testament either. Therefore, we have two theories about the original language of the New Testament. The author admits that the Seminary he attended drove home the belief that the Old Testament was written in Hebrew, except for a few spots. The New Testament was initially written in Koine Greek.

The writers' research has been searching for the original meaning of Scripture for many years. The methodology for this work is called "Ancient Bible Study Methods." The method was developed by Dr. Anne Davis of the Bible Learning University in Albuquerque, New Mexico. The author studied this method with Dr. Davis as his mentor. It became clear that the search for the original meaning of the Scriptures requires that the culture and language be examined. So, the author's methodology is Dr. Davis' work, plus his Ph.D. studies combining the method, culture, and language.

The language examination is easy for the Old Testament because it was written in Hebrew, and about one-half of Daniel is in Aramaic. It does not take long to realize that idioms and figures of speech in the Hebrew of the Old Testament revealed a lot about the people and situation of the day when the scrolls were written. The Targums were a valuable resource because they are the Aramaic translations the rabbis did for the people living outside of Judea. The rabbis added commentary to the Targums because they knew that some of the idioms and speech used in the Near East would not translate well into the different areas where the Jews lived.

The culture of the Near East has been essentially the same in many aspects since the days of Jesus. Many practices of Jesus' day are still in use today. The culture of the Jews of the Near East is built into the language. Many times an Aramaic or Hebrew word has a deep meaning that is only fully understood by natives who are living in that culture. The Old Testament is filled with cultural items that do not need to be spelled out because the people knew their culture at the author's time.

Suppose the New Testament in Koine Greek is a transliteration of the Aramaic. The culture, figures of speech, and idioms will be easy to identify when examining the Peshitta (the Aramaic version of the New Testament). Indeed many of the so-called difficult words of Jesus are not tricky when examined in the light of the culture of Jesus' day. An example is, "faith to move a mountain," Jesus said these words to His disciples. The church determined that this meant a complete faith in Jesus. From the western European Greek point of view, that makes sense. What else could it possibly mean?

"Faith to move a mountain" is an Aramaic idiomatic expression. What Jesus said to His followers when he said this is that his disciples needed to be faithful so that they could change the "government's view through their words." The governing body for Judaism resided on the top of a mountain. Jerusalem, with its Temple, was built on the top of Mount Zion, a very tall mountain. This idiom survived because the Aramaic Gospels were transliterated into Koine Greek. Numerous other examples support this position.

Suppose the culture and language idioms of Jesus' day can be found in the Koine Greek because it was transliterated. In that case, it supports the theory of the Aramaic versions being the original language of the Gospels and possibly even more.

The Aramaic Version of the New Testament

The Peshitta is the accepted Aramaic translation of the New Testament for many churches of the East. Peshitta means "simple, true, direct, and original." It is a collection of scrolls that were compiled in 150 CE. There were some revisions to the Peshitta in the fifth and sixth centuries. The Greek version of the New Testament is a transliteration of the Peshitta.[1]

For centuries, the Catholic church has been using the Latin version of the Bible, the Vulgate, and still uses it. The Vulgate was developed around 350 CE by Jerome by order of the Pope at that time. Erasmus (1466 – 1536) was the person who put together the Greek New Testament for the Catholic church.

"The New Testament, brought to light in the original Greek tongue, was compiled and made available for humanity to study and learn. Although working under and deeply associated with the Roman Catholic Church, the learned scholar declared his disagreement with those who wanted to keep the Scriptures from the common people. He said, "If only the farmer would sing something from them at his plow, the weaver moves his shuttle to their tune, the traveler lighten the boredom of his journey with Scriptural stories!" Little did he know, the work he was about to produce would change the world forever. This Greek New Testament, in printed form, would become the standard of the New Testament, launching the translations of Martin Luther and William Tyndale into the world. Thus, fulfilling his dream that all men would read the

---

[1] Rocco A. Errico and George M. Lamsa, *Aramaic Light on Galatians through Hebrews: A Commentary Based on Aramaic, the Language of Jesus, and Ancient near Eastern Customs* (Smyma, GA: Noohra Foundation, 2005).

Bible for themselves in their common language. His new "study Bible" had two main parts, the Greek text, and a revised Latin edition, which was more elegant and accurate than the traditional translation of Jerome's Latin Vulgate. Erasmus prefaced this monumental work of scholarship with an exhortation to Bible study. He proclaimed that the New Testament contains the "philosophy of Christ," simple and accessible teaching with the power to transform lives."[2]

The church recognized Erasmus' Greek New Testament in 1515 CE. The church in the Near East has been using the Peshitta as the original language of the New Testament since 150 CE. If the Greek New Testament was important to the church as an original language, then why did it adopt the Vulgate in 350 CE? The church should have adopted the Greek New Testament at the beginning.

The Peshitta, translated into English, is used to examine Paul's letters. The rest of the methodology that the author developed for Ancient Bible Study Methods is the framework of this research.

---

[2] "Erasmus Greek New Testament," Insight of the King, accessed February 18, 2022, https://www.insightoftheking.com/erasmus-greek-new-testament.html.

The Messianic Tradition Change

One problem for Peter and the Disciples was that they claimed Yeshua to be the Messiah that the prophets of the Hebrew Scriptures spoke of. However, Yeshua did not do what these traditions said. The main tradition was that the Messiah would destroy oppressive Romans and reinstate the Kingdom of Israel. Yeshua would then be declared the king and sit on David's throne in Jerusalem. That did not occur.

None of the messianic traditions of the day worked. So, what was the new movement going to do? They turned to the prophets and discovered Isaiah 50-53. These chapters are referred to as the Suffering Servant chapters. The Yeshua movement decided that the Suffering Servant was Yeshua. The portrayal of Yeshua's life does fit the Suffering Servant chapters. However, rabbinical interpretation then and now sees the Suffering Servant as the nation of Israel. Indeed, these chapters do describe the history of Israel. Nations have wanted to destroy the Jewish people since the time of Abraham.

The diaspora from the Babylonia Exile and the Assyrian invasions looked to squelch the Jewish people. The LORD promised that a remnant of the people would always survive. That is true throughout the 4,000-year history of the Jewish people. Many nations tried to destroy them, and the LORD intervened to ensure that a remnant of the people survived.

Paul must have been convinced in his encounter with Yeshua on the Damascus road that Yeshua was the Suffering Servant. It is clear from Paul's writings that he did believe this. For Paul, the Messiah was the Spiritual Messiah that the Kabbalah spoke. The

Kabbalah says that there will be two Messiahs. This is based on Zachariah 9:9. The first Messiah is Messiah ben Joseph. This Messiah was to restore the Kingdom of Heaven, which is a spiritual Kingdom. The second Messiah will be Messiah ben David. This Messiah was to restore the Kingdom of Israel. The Midrash from the Kabbalah did not state that the Messiah was two different souls.

The Kabbalah

There is a large amount of material in print about the Kabbalah. The Kabbalah referred to is Moses's Secret Work from Mount Sinai. Legends say Moses received three items on Mount Sinai when he met the LORD. The first is the written Law. The written Law is called the Torah. The second is the oral law. The oral law was put into a written form around 200 CE called the Mishnah. The third is the secret law called the Kabbalah. The secrets of the Kabbalah are based on the Torah and were written down around 200 CE. The main books of the Kabbalah are the Zohar and the Book of Creation.

Many of Yeshua's statements have Kabbalah undertones. Yeshua would have known the Kabbalah. Paul would have known the basics, at least, of the Kabbalah because of his religious education and training.

There are Kabbalistic ideas in the Gospels and Paul's letters. Kabbalistic verses will be highlighted in the chapters of the letters.

Methodology

The methodology employed is to use "Ancient Bible Study Methods" integrated with Jesus's day's customs and culture to examine the Hebrew and Christian Scriptures, thus gathering a more in-depth understanding by learning the Scriptures in the way the people of Jesus's day did.

I have titled the methodology of analyzing a passage of Scripture in a Hebraic manner the "Process of Discovery." The author developed this methodology, which brings together various linguistic and cultural understanding areas. There are several sections to the process, and not all the parts apply to every passage of Scripture. The overall result of developing this process is to give the reader a framework for studying the Word in more depth.

The "Process of Discovery" starts with a Scripture passage. An examination of the linguistic structure of the passage is next. The linguistic structure includes parallelism, chiastic structures, and repetition. Formatting the passage in its linguistic form allows the reader to visualize what the first century C.E. listener was hearing. Their corresponding sections label the chiasms, for example, A, B, C, B', A.' Not all passages of the Scriptures have a poetic form.

The next step is to "question the narrative." The narrative process of questioning the narrative assumes the reader knows nothing about the passage. Therefore, the questions go from the simple to the complex. The next task is to identify any linguistic patterns. Linguistic patterns include, but are not limited to, irony, simile, metaphor, symbolism, idioms, hyperbole, figurative language, personification, and allegory.

A review of any translation inconsistencies discovered between the English NAU version and either the Hebrew or Greek versions is done. There are times when a Hebrew or Greek word is translated in more than one way. Inconsistencies also can be created by the translation committee, which may have decided to use traditional language instead of the actual translation. The decision of the translation committee is in the Preface or Introduction to the Bible. Perhaps some of the inconsistencies were intentionally added to convey some deeper meaning. An examination for every discrepancy is done.

The passage is analyzed for any echoes of the Hebrew Scriptures in the Christian Scriptures. An echo occurs using a passage from the Hebrew Scriptures in the Christian Scriptures.[3] Also, echoes are found when Torah (Genesis through Deuteronomy) passages are used in other Hebrew Bible books. Cross-references in the Scripture are references from one verse to another verse, which can help the reader understand the verse.

The names of persons mentioned in the passage are listed. Many of the Hebrew names have meaning and may be associated with places or actions. Jewish parents used to name their children based on what they felt God had in store for their child. An example of this is Abraham, whose original name was Abram and was changed to mean eternal father (God changed Abram's name to Abraham, indicating a function he was to perform). When the Hebrew Bible gives names, many occurrences mean something unique. The same importance can occur for the names of places. The time it takes to travel between locations can supply insight into the event.

---

[3] Mitzvot are the 613 commandments found in the Torah that please God. There are positive and negative commandments. The list was first development by Maimonides. The full list can be found at: http://www.jewfaq.org/613.htm.

Keyphrases are identified in verses when they are essential to understanding that passage. There are no rules for selecting the keywords. Searching for other occurrences of the keywords in Scripture in a concordance is necessary to understand the Word's usage; this must be done in either Hebrew or Greek, not in English. A classic Hebraic approach is to find the usage of a word in the Scripture by finding other verses that contain the Word. The usage of a word in its original language is discovered by searching the Scripture in the language of the Word. Verses that contain the Word are identified, and a pattern for the usage of the Word is discovered. Each verse is examined to see what the usage of the Word is, which may reveal a model for the Word's usage. The first usage of the Word in the Scripture, primarily if used in the Torah, is essential for Hebrew words. For the Greek words, the Christian Scriptures are used to determine the Word usage in the Scripture. Sometimes, it can be very helpful to find the equivalent Greek Word in the Septuagint and then analyze its Hebrew usage.

The Rules of Hillel are used when applicable. Hillel was a Torah scholar who lived shortly before Jesus's day. Hillel developed several rules for Torah students to interpret the Scriptures, which refer to halachic Midrash. In several cases, these rules are helpful in the analysis of the Scripture.

The cultural implications from the writing period are done after the linguistic analysis is completed. The culture is crucial because it is not explicitly referenced in the biblical narratives, as indicated earlier.

From the linguistic analysis and the cultural understanding, it is possible to obtain a deeper meaning of the Scripture beyond the plain text's literal meaning. That is what the listeners of Jesus's time were doing. They put linguistics and culture together without even having to contemplate it.

The analysis will lead to a set of findings explaining what the passage meant in Jesus's day. Most of the time, the Hebraic analysis leads to the desire for more in-depth analysis to fully understand what Jesus was talking about or what was happening to Him. Whatever the result, a new, more in-depth understanding of the Scripture is obtained.

The components of the Process of Discovery are:

Language

Process of Discovery

Linguistics Section

Linguistic Structure

Discussion

Questioning the Passage

Verse Comparison of citations or proof text

Translation Inconsistencies

Biblical Personalities

Biblical Locations

Phrase Study

Linguistic Echoes

Rules of Hillel

Culture Section

Discussion

Questioning the passage

Cultural Echoes

Culture and Linguistics Section

Discussion

Thoughts

Reflections

Only the applicable sections are included in this document.

Introduction to the Letter

This letter was probably written around 51 CE. There is some scholarly debate whether Paul wrote the letter. Either way, it is a part of the New Testament and needs to be treated with respect. Paul was traveling with his companions, Silvanus and Timothy. The letter advises the congregation to be cautious of those who are deceiving, causing trouble, and falsely prophesying the return of Yeshua. A lot of forged letters were being circulated throughout the proto-orthodox church, claiming to have been written by Paul.

Paul encouraged the congregation to remain loyal to the truth of the Gospel, according to Yeshua. Paul tried to clear up some misunderstandings about the coming of Yeshua, which he mentioned in his first letter to the congregation.

Chapter One

Language

Peshitta	New American Standard 1995
2Th. 1:1 Paul and Sylvanus and Timothy, to the church of the Thessalonians, which is in God our Father and our Lord Jesus the Messiah: **2** Grace be with you, and peace, from God our Father, and from our Lord Jesus the Messiah. **3** We are bound to give thanks to God always, on your account, my brethren, as it is proper; because your faith groweth exceedingly, and, in you all, the love of each for his fellow increaseth. **4** Insomuch that we also boast of you in the churches of God, on account of your faith, and your patience in all the persecution and trials that ye endure; **5** for a demonstration of the righteous judgment of God; that ye may be worthy of his kingdom, on account of which ye suffer. **6** And since it is a righteous thing with God, to recompense trouble to them that trouble you: **7** and you, who are the troubled, he will vivify, with us, at the manifestation of our Lord Jesus the Messiah from heaven, with the host of his angels; **8** when he will execute vengeance, with the burning of fire, on them that know not God, and on them that acknowledge not the gospel of our Lord Jesus the Messiah. **9** For these will be recompensed with the judgment of eternal destruction, from the presence of our Lord, and from the glory of his power; **10** when he shall come to be glorified in his saints, and to display his wonders in his faithful ones; for our	**2Th. 1:1** *a*Paul and *b*Silvanus and *c*Timothy, *Thanksgiving for Faith and Perseverance* To the *d*church of the Thessalonians in God our Father and the Lord Jesus Christ: **2** *a*Grace to you and peace from God the Father and the Lord Jesus Christ. **2Th. 1:3** We ought always *a*to give thanks to God for you, *b*brethren, as is *only* fitting, because your faith is greatly enlarged, and the *c*love of each one of you toward one another grows *ever* greater; **4** therefore, we ourselves *a*speak proudly of you among *b*the churches of God for your ¹perseverance and faith *b*in the midst of all your persecutions and afflictions which you endure. **5** *This is* a *a*plain indication of God's righteous judgment so that you will be *b*considered worthy of the kingdom of God, for which indeed you are suffering. **6** ¹For after all *a*it is *only* just ²for God to repay with affliction those who afflict you, **7** and *to give* relief to you who are afflicted ¹and to us as well ²*a*when the Lord Jesus will be revealed *b*from heaven *c*with ³His mighty angels *d*in flaming fire, **8** dealing out retribution to those who *a*do not know God and to those who *b*do not obey the gospel of our Lord Jesus. **9** These will pay the penalty of *a*eternal destruction, *b*away

testimony concerning you, will be believed, in that day. **11** Therefore we pray for you, at all times; that God would make you worthy of your calling, and would fill you with all readiness for good deeds, and with the works of faith by power; **12** so that the name of our Lord Jesus the Messiah, may be glorified in you, (and) ye also in him; according to the grace of God, and of our Lord Jesus the Messiah.	from the presence of the Lord and from the glory of His power, **10** when He comes to be *a*glorified [1]in His [2]saints on that *b*day, and to be marveled at among all who have believed — for our *c*testimony to you was believed. **11** To this end also we *a*pray for you always, that our God will [1b]count you worthy of your *c*calling, and fulfill every desire for *d*goodness and the *e*work of faith with power, **12** so that the *a*name of our Lord Jesus will be glorified in you, and you in Him, according to the grace of our God and *the* Lord Jesus Christ.

References to the New American Standard 1995

2Thessalonians 1:1
[a]1 Thess 1:1
[b]2 Cor 1:19
[c]Acts 16:1
[d]Acts 17:1; 1 Thess 1:1

2Thessalonians 1:2
[a]Rom 1:7

2Thessalonians 1:3
[a]Rom 1:8; Eph 5:20; 1 Thess 1:2; 2 Thess 2:13
[b]1 Thess 4:1; 2 Thess 2:1
[c]1 Thess 3:12

2Thessalonians 1:4
[1]Or *steadfastness*
[a]2 Cor 7:4; 1 Thess 2:19
[b]1 Cor 7:17; 1 Thess 2:14

2Thessalonians 1:5
[a]Phil 1:28
[b]Luke 20:35; 2 Thess 1:11

2Thessalonians 1:6
[1]Lit *If indeed*
[2]Or *in the sight of*
[a]Ex 23:22; Col 3:25; Heb 6:10

2Thessalonians 1:7
[1]Lit *along with us*
[2]Lit *at the revelation of the Lord Jesus*
[3]Lit *the angels of His power*
[a]Luke 17:30
[b]1 Thess 4:16
[c]Jude 14
[d]Ex 3:2; 19:18; Is 66:15; Ezek 1:13; Dan 7:9; Matt 25:41; 1 Cor 3:13; Heb 10:27; 12:29;
2 Pet 3:7; Jude 7; Rev 14:10

2Thessalonians 1:8
[a]Gal 4:8
[b]Rom 2:8

2Thessalonians 1:9
[a]Phil 3:19; 1 Thess 5:3
[b]Is 2:10, 19, 21; 2 Thess 2:8

2Thessalonians 1:10
[1]Or *in the persons of*
[2]Or *holy ones*
[a]Is 49:3; John 17:10; 1 Thess 2:12
[b]Is 2:11ff; 1 Cor 3:13
[c]1 Cor 1:6; 1 Thess 2:1

2Thessalonians 1:11
[1]Or *make*
[a]Col 1:9
[b]2 Thess 1:5
[c]Rom 11:29
[d]Rom 15:14
[e]1 Thess 1:3

2Thessalonians 1:12
[a]Is 24:15; 66:5; Mal 1:11; Phil 2:9ff

Koine Greek

2Th. 1:0 ΠΡΟΣ ΘΕΣΣΑΛΟΝΙΚΕΙΣ Β

2Th. 1:1   Παυλος και Σιλουανος και Τιμοθεος τη εκκλησια Θεσσαλονικεων εν θεω πατρι ημων και κυριω Ιησου Χριστω, [2] χαρις υμιν και ειρηνη απο θεου πατρος ημων και κυριου Ιησου Χριστου.

2Th. 1:3   Ευχαριστειν οφειλομεν τω θεω παντοτε περι υμων, αδελφοι, καθως αξιον εστιν, οτι υπεραυξανει η πιστις υμων και πλεοναζει η αγαπη ενος εκαστου παντων υμων εις αλληλους, [4] ωστε αυτους ημας εν υμιν εγκαυχασθαι εν ταις εκκλησιαις του θεου υπερ της υπομονης υμων και πιστεως εν πασιν τοις διωγμοις υμων και ταις θλιψεσιν αις ανεχεσθε, [5] ενδειγμα της δικαιας κρισεως του θεου εις το καταξιωθηναι υμας της βασιλειας του θεου, υπερ ης και πασχετε, [6] ειπερ δικαιον παρα θεω ανταποδουναι τοις θλιβουσιν υμας θλιψιν [7] και υμιν τοις θλιβομενοις ανεσιν μεθ' ημων, εν τη αποκαλυψει του κυριου Ιησου απ' ουρανου μετ' αγγελων δυναμεως αυτου [8] εν πυρι φλογος, διδοντος εκδικησιν τοις μη ειδοσιν θεον και τοις μη υπακουουσιν τω ευαγγελιω του κυριου ημων Ιησου, [9] οιτινες δικην τισουσιν ολεθρον αιωνιον απο προσωπου του κυριου και απο της δοξης της ισχυος αυτου, [10] οταν ελθη ενδοξασθηναι εν τοις αγιοις αυτου και θαυμασθηναι εν πασιν τοις πιστευσασιν, οτι επιστευθη το μαρτυριον ημων εφ' υμας, εν τη ημερα εκεινη. [11] Εις ο και προσευχομεθα παντοτε περι υμων, ινα υμας αξιωση της κλησεως ο θεος ημων και πληρωση πασαν ευδοκιαν αγαθωσυνης και εργον πιστεως εν δυναμει, [12] οπως ενδοξασθη το ονομα του κυριου ημων Ιησου εν υμιν, και υμεις εν αυτω, κατα την χαριν του θεου ημων και κυριου Ιησου Χριστου.

Language

  Process of Discovery

    Linguistics Section

      Linguistic Structure

2Th. 1:1 [a]Paul and [b]Silvanus and [c]Timothy, To the [d]church of the Thessalonians in God our Father and the Lord Jesus Christ: **2** [a]Grace to you and peace from God the Father and the Lord Jesus Christ.

A [3] We ought always [a]to give thanks to God for you, [b]brethren, as is *only* fitting, because your faith is greatly enlarged, and the [c]love of each one of you toward one another grows *ever* greater;

  B [4] therefore, we ourselves [a]speak proudly of you among [b]the churches of God for your [1]perseverance and faith [b]in the midst of all your persecutions and afflictions which you endure. **5** *This is* a [a]plain indication of God's righteous judgment so that you will be [b]considered worthy of the kingdom of God, for which indeed you are suffering.

    C [6] [1]For after all [a]it is *only* just [2]for God to repay with affliction those who afflict you, **7** and *to give* relief to you who are afflicted [1]and to us as well [2a]when the Lord Jesus will be revealed [b]from heaven [c]with [3]His mighty angels [d]in flaming fire, **8** dealing out retribution to those who [a]do not know God and to those who [b]do not obey the gospel of our Lord Jesus. **9** These will pay the penalty of [a]eternal destruction, [b]away from the presence of the Lord and from the glory of His power,

  B' [10] when He comes to be [a]glorified [1]in His [2]saints on that [b]day, and to be marveled at among all who have believed — for our [c]testimony to you was believed.

A' [11] To this end also we [a]pray for you always, that our God will [1b]count you worthy of your [c]calling, and fulfill every desire for [d]goodness and the [e]work of faith with power, **12** so that the [a]name of our Lord Jesus will be glorified in you, and you in Him, according to the grace of our God and *the* Lord Jesus Christ.

Discussion

This chapter is a simple chiasm being A-B-C. In the introduction to the letter, Paul commends the congregation for staying together in the sight of persecutions.

Questioning the Passage

1. How does the author know that the congregation loves one another? (v. 3)

    Paul is making a conjecture at this point. He does not know what the attitudes of the people in the congregation are. However, he believed that if the people were imitating the values of Yeshua's Gospel, then they would certain be taking care of each other. This is a compliment of praise before the condemnations.

2. What are persecutions and afflictions? (v. 4)

    The persecutions and afflictions were coming from two directions. There was the Jewish religious leadership, who was not happy that Yeshua's teaching was being spread. Also, being a "new" religion, they came under the scrutiny of the Roman government.

3. What is the righteous judgment of God? (v. 5)

    The people of the congregation were enduring the wrath being thrown at them. Since they were surviving the onslaught, Paul told them they were filled with the righteous judgment of God. In other words, the people were following the ways of the LORD and would be protected and taken into Heaven because they knew and followed the truth.

4. What is the Kingdom of God? (v. 5)

    The Kingdom of God is a collection of the people on earth who believe in the words and actions of Yeshua. Also, they must believe that Yeshua is the Messiah that the LORD promised to send his people. When in the kingdom, a person is shielded from the evils and sins of the world.

5. What is the meaning of verses 6, 7, 8, 9)?

    These four verses are Paul's way of describing Yeshua's parable of the wheat and tares.

    Matt. 13:24 Jesus presented another parable to them, saying, "*The kingdom of heaven [1]may be compared to a man who sowed good seed in his field. [25] "But while his men were sleeping, his enemy came and sowed [1]tares among the wheat, and went away. [26] "But when the [1]wheat sprouted and bore grain, then the tares became evident also. [27] "The slaves of the landowner came and said to him, 'Sir, did you not sow good seed in your field? [1]How then does it have tares?' [28] "And he said to them, 'An [1]enemy has done this!' The slaves *said to him, 'Do you want us, then, to go and gather them up?' [29] "But he *said, 'No; for while you are gathering up the tares, you may uproot the wheat with them. [30] 'Allow both to grow together until the harvest; and in the time of the harvest I will say to the reapers, "First gather up the tares and bind them in bundles to burn them up; but [a]gather the wheat into my barn."'"

    According to Paul, when Yeshua returns, the faithful will rejoice with him. However, the disobedient and sinners will suffer great torment. These people have exchanged truth for the error of believing in darkness (sinning).

6. What is eternal destruction? (v. 9)

   Eternal destruction is the disconnect from the LORD. It was believed that if a soul was sent to Hell that the soul could never communicate or connect with the LORD. Therefore, the soul was lost forever.

7. What is the meaning of verse ten?

   To have Yeshua glorified with a person means that through the person, the teachings of Yeshua would become known.

8. What is the work of faith with power? (v. 11)

   Faith with power is exhibited when the outside forces of society attack the congregation. The people have the power through faith to resist and turn back any aggressors.

9. What is the grace of God? (v. 12)

   The grace of God comes from the unity of the LORD and Jesus Christ. Some denominations (especially orthodoxy) would say that the Holy Spirit is the unity of God and Christ. This grace allows the followers of Yeshua to see and experience the love of the LORD.

10. What is the grace of the Lord Jesus Christ? (v. 12)

    Paul implies that the grace of God and of Jesus are the same and one.

Biblical Personalities

1. Paul

   Paul, also known as Saint Paul or the Apostle Paul, was a significant figure in early Christianity and one of the most influential writers and missionaries in the

New Testament of the Bible. He was born as Saul of Tarsus, likely around AD 5-10, in the city of Tarsus, which is in modern-day Turkey. He is traditionally believed to have died around AD 64-67.

Paul's life underwent a dramatic transformation. Originally, he was a Pharisee and a persecutor of early Christians. According to the Bible, he experienced a profound conversion on the road to Damascus when he encountered a vision of Jesus Christ. This event led to his acceptance of Christianity and his subsequent missionary work to spread the Christian faith.

Some key points about Paul's life and contributions:

1. Missionary Work: Paul undertook several missionary journeys throughout the Mediterranean region, preaching and establishing Christian communities. His journeys are recorded in the Book of Acts in the New Testament.

2. Writings: Paul is known for his letters, or epistles, which form a significant portion of the New Testament. These letters include Romans, Corinthians (1 and 2), Galatians, Ephesians, Philippians, Colossians, Thessalonians (1 and 2), Timothy (1 and 2), Titus, and Philemon. These writings provide theological teachings and guidance to early Christian communities.

3. Theology: Paul's theological contributions had a profound impact on Christian doctrine. He emphasized the grace of God, salvation through faith in Jesus Christ, and the importance of love and unity within the Christian community.

4. Role in Early Church: Paul played a crucial role in shaping the early Christian Church and its understanding of the relationship between Judaism and Christianity. He argued for the inclusion of Gentiles (non-Jews) in the Christian community without requiring them to observe Jewish laws and customs.

5. Martyrdom: Tradition holds that Paul was martyred in Rome under the Emperor Nero, likely by beheading, around AD 64-67. His martyrdom is not explicitly recorded in the New Testament.

Overall, Paul's teachings and missionary efforts had a lasting influence on the development of Christianity, and his letters continue to be studied and revered by Christians worldwide.

2. Silvanus

Silvanus, also known as Silas, was a figure mentioned in the New Testament of the Bible. He is most prominently featured in the Acts of the Apostles and several of the Pauline epistles. Silvanus was a Christian missionary and companion to the Apostle Paul during his missionary journeys.

In the Book of Acts, Silvanus is first introduced as a fellow Christian in the early church in Jerusalem. He later joined Paul on his second missionary journey, during which he played a significant role in delivering the decisions of the Jerusalem Council to the churches in Antioch and Syria (Acts 15:22).

Silvanus is mentioned as a co-author or sender in some of the Pauline epistles, including 1 Thessalonians, 2 Thessalonians, and 1 Peter. In these letters, his name is often mentioned alongside Paul or Peter, indicating his involvement in spreading the Christian message and assisting in the establishment of Christian communities.

While Silvanus is not one of the central figures of the Bible, he played a supportive role in the early Christian church and was instrumental in conveying important messages and letters among various Christian communities.

3. Timothy

    Timothy, also known as Timothy of Lystra, was a prominent figure in the New Testament of the Bible. He was a young Christian and a close companion and disciple of the Apostle Paul. Timothy is mentioned in several New Testament books, particularly in the letters written by Paul.

    Here are some key aspects of Timothy's role in the Bible:

    1. **Background**: Timothy was from Lystra, a city in the region of Galatia (modern-day Turkey). His mother, Eunice, and grandmother, Lois, are mentioned as believers in the Christian faith. Timothy was likely influenced by them in his Christian upbringing.

    2. **Companion of Paul**: Timothy first comes to prominence when Paul visits Lystra during his second missionary journey (Acts 16:1-3). Impressed by Timothy's character and reputation among the local believers, Paul invited him to join his missionary team.

    3. **Paul's Letters to Timothy**: Paul wrote two pastoral letters to Timothy, known as 1 Timothy and 2 Timothy, which are part of the New Testament.

These letters were intended to provide guidance and instruction to Timothy as a young leader in the early Christian church. They cover various aspects of leadership, doctrine, and conduct within the Christian community.

4. **Leadership Roles**: Timothy played a significant role in overseeing and shepherding the Christian communities in Ephesus and other places. He was entrusted with responsibilities related to teaching, correcting false teachings, and appointing church leaders.

5. **Close Relationship with Paul**: Paul held Timothy in high regard and referred to him as his "true child in the faith" (1 Timothy 1:2). Timothy traveled with Paul on his missionary journeys and served as his representative in various situations.

Timothy is an important figure in the early Christian church, and his partnership with the Apostle Paul contributed significantly to the spread of Christianity in the first century. The letters addressed to him by Paul provide valuable insights into early Christian theology and leadership within the church.

Biblical Locations [4]

[4] 1. Bing, accessed September 10, 2023, https://www.bing.com/images.

Culture Section

Discussion

The congregation considered persecution and suffering for Yeshua's teachings as a righteous act. Christians glorified the name of Yeshua when they suffered. Yeshua said that blessed are they which are persecuted for righteousness' sake, for theirs is the kingdom of heaven. The early life of these Yeshua congregations was not an easy one. The Yeshua House churches could be in danger from Roman officials and other Mithras House churches. In the Roman Empire, only two religions were openly accepted. The Mithras religion and Judaism were the two recognized religions. Other religious groups were persecuted. Christians of those days were quite content to declare that they were not a sect of Judaism. This caused oppression from the government and the accepted religion of the Empire.

If the Jewish congregations had only believed in Yeshua as the Messiah, they would have been left alone by the Roman government. However, the Jewish leadership tried to destroy them. Paul, when he was Saul, was one of those officials' commissions to place Yeshua's followers in jail. Yeshua's original disciples and followers were dying off during the years after Yeshua died. The Mithras conversion was collecting steam. It was a matter of time when the first remnants of Jewish believers were gone.

In the beginning of the persecutions, some community members felt their lives were as good as or better before they converted to Christianity. These men and women would have desired the leave the congregation. This would have weakened the church to where it could not have survived. Therefore, Paul wrote in his letter that for one to become a saint, one had to suffer because one was a follower of Yeshua. This idea is still a part of today's theology, which is quite unfortunate.

Questioning the passage

1. What does fire metaphorically express? (v. 7)

   Fire was often used as a metaphor to express "mental torment and prolonged anguish." In Babylon, criminals were punished by burning.

   Daniel [15] "Now if you are ready, [a]at the moment you hear the sound of the horn, flute, [1]lyre, trigon, psaltery and bagpipe and all kinds of music, to fall down and worship the image that I have made, *very well*. But if you do not worship, you will [2]immediately be [b]cast into the midst of a furnace of blazing fire; and [c]what god is there who can deliver you out of my hands?"

   During the Babylonian Exile, fire was feared more than anything else. Fire would burn forests and cities. Fire also can purify metal. It is a metaphor that can be used in two different ways. In this passage, it is the metaphor for fear and destruction.

Thoughts

It is sad when pastors today say that a person is not qualified to become a pastor, a messenger from the LORD, unless they have suffered in life. Today, it is unnecessary to suffer in the manner the people in Thessalonia did. Yeshua calls all kinds of people to be his ambassadors. If this attitude is maintained in the world, eventually there will not be enough pastors to serve all the churches.

Chapter Two

Language

Peshitta	New American Standard 1995
2Th. 2:1 But we entreat of you, my brethren, in regard to the coming of our Lord Jesus the Messiah, and in respect to our being congregated unto him, **2** that ye be not soon agitated in your mind, nor be troubled, neither by word, nor by spirit, nor by letter, as coming from us, that lo, the day of our Lord is at hand. **3** Let no one deceive you in any way; because [that day will not come], unless there previously come a defection, and that man of sin be revealed, the son of perdition; **4** who is an opposer, and exalteth himself above all that is called God and Worshipful; so that he also sitteth in the temple of God, as a God, and displayeth himself, as if he were God. **5** Do ye not remember, that, when I was with you, I told you these things? **6** And now, ye know what hindereth his being manifested in his time. **7** For the mystery of the evil One already beginneth to be operative: and only, if that which now hindereth shall be taken from the midst; **8** then at length will that evil One be revealed; whom our Lord Jesus will consume by the breath of his mouth, and will bring to naught by the visibility of his advent. **9** For the coming of that [evil One], is the working of Satan, with all power, and signs, and lying wonders, **10** and with all the deceptiveness of iniquity, in them that perish; because they did not receive the	**2Th. 2:1** Now we request you, [a]brethren, with regard to the [1b]coming of our Lord Jesus Christ and our [c]gathering together to Him, **2** that you not be quickly shaken from your [1]composure or be disturbed either by a [a]spirit or a [2b]message or a [c]letter as if from us, to the effect that [d]the day of the Lord [e]has come. **3** [a]Let no one in any way deceive you, for *it will not come* unless the [1b]apostasy comes first, and the [c]man of lawlessness is revealed, the [d]son of destruction, **4** who opposes and exalts himself above [1a]every so-called god or object of worship, so that he takes his seat in the temple of God, [b]displaying himself as being God. **5** Do you not remember that [a]while I was still with you, I was telling you these things? **6** And you know [a]what restrains him now, so that in his time he will be revealed. **7** For [a]the mystery of lawlessness is already at work; only [b]he who now restrains *will do so* until he is taken out of the way. **8** Then that lawless one [a]will be revealed whom the Lord will slay [b]with the breath of His mouth and bring to an end by the [c]appearance of His [1]coming; **9** *that is,* the one whose [1]coming is in accord with the activity of [a]Satan, with all power and [2b]signs and false wonders, **10** and with [1]all the deception of wickedness for [a]those who perish, because they did not receive the love of [b]the truth so as to

love of the truth, by which they might have life. **11** Therefore God will send upon them the operation of deception, that they may believe a lie; **12** and that they all may be condemned, who believe not the truth, but have pleasure in iniquity. **13** But we are bound to give thanks to God always, on your account, my brethren beloved of our Lord, that God hath from the beginning chosen you unto life, through sanctification of the Spirit, and through faith in the truth. **14** For unto these it was, that God called you by our preaching; that ye might be the glory to our Lord Jesus the Messiah. **15** Therefore, my brethren, be established, and persevere in the precepts which ye have been taught, whether by word or by our epistle. **16** And may our Lord Jesus the Messiah himself, and God our Father, who hath loved us, and given us everlasting consolation and a good hope through his grace, **17** comfort your hearts, and establish [you] in every good word, and in every good work.

be saved. **11** For this reason *a*God [1]will send upon them [2]a *b*deluding influence so that they will believe [3]what is false, **12** in order that they all may be [1]judged who *a*did not believe the truth, but [2b]took pleasure in wickedness.

2Th. 2:13 *a*But we should always give thanks to God for you, *b*brethren beloved by the Lord, because *c*God has chosen you [1]from the beginning *d*for salvation [2e]through sanctification [3]by the Spirit and faith in the truth. **14** It was for this He *a*called you through *b*our gospel, [1]that you may gain the glory of our Lord Jesus Christ. **15** So then, brethren, *a*stand firm and *b*hold to the traditions which you were taught, whether *c*by word *of mouth* or *d*by letter [1]from us.

2Th. 2:16 *a*Now may our Lord Jesus Christ *a*Himself and God our Father, who has *b*loved us and given us eternal comfort and *c*good hope by grace, **17** *a*comfort and *b*strengthen your hearts in every good work and word.

References to the New American Standard 1995

2Thessalonians 2:1
[1]Or *presence*
[a]2 Thess 1:3
[b]1 Thess 2:19
[c]Mark 13:27; 1 Thess 4:15-17

2Thessalonians 2:2
[1]Lit *mind*
[2]Lit *word*
[a]1 Cor 14:32; 1 John 4:1
[b]1 Thess 5:2; 2 Thess 2:15
[c]2 Thess 3:17
[d]1 Cor 1:8
[e]1 Cor 7:26

2Thessalonians 2:3
[1]Or *falling away* from the faith
[a]Eph 5:6
[b]1 Tim 4:1
[c]Dan 7:25; 8:25; 11:36; 2 Thess 2:8; Rev 13:5ff
[d]John 17:12

2Thessalonians 2:4
[1]Or *everyone who is called God*
[a]1 Cor 8:5
[b]Is 14:14; Ezek 28:2

2Thessalonians 2:5
[a]1 Thess 3:4

2Thessalonians 2:6
[a]2 Thess 2:7

2Thessalonians 2:7
[a]Rev 17:5, 7
[b]2 Thess 2:6

2Thessalonians 2:8

[1]Or *presence*
[a]Dan 7:25; 8:25; 11:36; 2 Thess 2:3; Rev 13:5ff
[b]Is 11:4; Rev 2:16; 19:15
[c]1 Tim 6:14; 2 Tim 1:10; 4:1, 8; Titus 2:13

2Thessalonians 2:9

[1]Or *presence*
[2]Or *attesting miracles*
[a]Matt 4:10
[b]Matt 24:24; John 4:48

2Thessalonians 2:10

[1]Or *every deception*
[a]1 Cor 1:18
[b]2 Thess 2:12, 13

2Thessalonians 2:11

[1]Lit *is sending*
[2]Lit *an activity of error*
[3]Or *the lie*
[a]1 Kin 22:22; Rom 1:28
[b]1 Thess 2:3; 2 Tim 4:4

2Thessalonians 2:12

[1]Or *condemned*
[2]Or *approved*
[a]Rom 2:8
[b]Rom 1:32; 1 Cor 13:6

2Thessalonians 2:13

[1]One early ms reads *first fruits*
[2]Lit *in*
[3]Lit *of*
[a]2 Thess 1:3
[b]1 Thess 1:4
[c]Eph 1:4ff
[d]1 Cor 1:21; 1 Thess 2:12; 5:9; 1 Pet 1:5
[e]1 Thess 4:7; 1 Pet 1:2

2Thessalonians 2:14

[1]Lit *to the gaining of*

[a]1 Thess 2:12
[b]1 Thess 1:5

2Thessalonians 2:15

[1]Lit *of*
[a]1 Cor 16:13
[b]1 Cor 11:2; 2 Thess 3:6
[c]2 Thess 2:2

2Thessalonians 2:16

[a]1 Thess 3:11
[b]John 3:16
[c]Titus 3:7; 1 Pet 1:3

2Thessalonians 2:17

[a]1 Thess 3:2, 13
[b]2 Thess 3:3

2Thessalonians 3:1

[1]Lit *run*
[a]1 Thess 4:1
[b]1 Thess 5:25
[c]1 Thess 1:8

Koine Greek

2Th. 2:1 Ερωτωμεν δε υμας, αδελφοι, υπερ της παρουσιας του κυριου ημων Ιησου Χριστου και ημων επισυναγωγης επ' αυτον [2] εις το μη ταχεως σαλευθηναι υμας απο του νοος μηδε θροεισθαι, μητε δια πνευματος μητε δια λογου μητε δι' επιστολης ως δι' ημων, ως οτι ενεστηκεν η ημερα του κυριου·

2Th. 2:3 Μη τις υμας εξαπατηση κατα μηδενα τροπον. οτι εαν μη ελθη η αποστασια πρωτον και αποκαλυφθη ο ανθρωπος της ανομιας, ο υιος της απωλειας, [4] ο αντικειμενος και υπεραιρομενος επι παντα λεγομενον θεον η σεβασμα, ωστε αυτον εις τον ναον του θεου καθισαι αποδεικνυντα εαυτον οτι εστιν θεος. [5] Ου μνημονευετε οτι ετι ων προς υμας ταυτα ελεγον υμιν; [6] και νυν το κατεχον οιδατε εις το αποκαλυφθηναι αυτον εν τω εαυτου καιρω. [7] το γαρ μυστηριον ηδη ενεργειται της ανομιας· μονον ο κατεχων αρτι εως εκ μεσου γενηται. [8] και τοτε αποκαλυφθησεται ο ανομος, ον ο κυριος Ιησους ανελει τω πνευματι του στοματος αυτου και καταργησει τη επιφανεια της παρουσιας αυτου, [9] ου εστιν η παρουσια κατ' ενεργειαν του σατανα εν παση δυναμει και σημειοις και τερασιν ψευδους [10] και εν παση απατη αδικιας τοις απολλυμενοις, ανθ' ων την αγαπην της αληθειας ουκ εδεξαντο εις το σωθηναι αυτους. [11] και δια τουτο πεμπει αυτοις ο θεος ενεργειαν πλανης εις το πιστευσαι αυτους τω ψευδει, [12] ινα κριθωσιν παντες οι μη πιστευσαντες τη αληθεια αλλ' ευδοκησαντες τη αδικια.

2Th. 2:13 Ημεις δε οφειλομεν ευχαριστειν τω θεω παντοτε περι υμων, αδελφοι ηγαπημενοι υπο κυριου, οτι ειλατο υμας ο θεος απαρχην εις σωτηριαν εν αγιασμω πνευματος και πιστει αληθειας, [14] εις ο και εκαλεσεν υμας δια του ευαγγελιου ημων εις περιποιησιν δοξης του κυριου ημων Ιησου Χριστου.

2Th. 2:15 Αρα ουν, αδελφοι, στηκετε και κρατειτε τας παραδοσεις ας εδιδαχθητε ειτε δια λογου ειτε δι' επιστολης ημων. [16] Αυτος δε ο κυριος ημων Ιησους Χριστος και ο θεος ο πατηρ ημων ο αγαπησας ημας και δους παρακλησιν αιωνιαν και ελπιδα αγαθην εν χαριτι, [17] παρακαλεσαι υμων τας καρδιας και στηριξαι εν παντι εργω και λογω αγαθω.

Language

  Process of Discovery

    Linguistics Section

     Linguistic Structure

A   [1] Now we request you, [a]brethren, with regard to the [1b]coming of our Lord Jesus Christ and our [c]gathering together to Him, **2** that you not be quickly shaken from your [1]composure or be disturbed either by a [a]spirit or a [2b]message or a [c]letter as if from us, to the effect that [d]the day of the Lord [e]has come.

> **B** **3** [a]Let no one in any way deceive you, for *it will not come* unless the [1b]apostasy comes first, and the [c]man of lawlessness is revealed, the [d]son of destruction, **4** who opposes and exalts himself above [1a]every so-called god or object of worship, so that he takes his seat in the temple of God, [b]displaying himself as being God.
>
> > **C** **5** Do you not remember that [a]while I was still with you, I was telling you these things? **6** And you know [a]what restrains him now, so that in his time he will be revealed. **7** For [a]the mystery of lawlessness is already at work; only [b]he who now restrains *will do so* until he is taken out of the way. **8** Then that lawless one [a]will be revealed whom the Lord will slay [b]with the breath of His mouth and bring to an end by the [c]appearance of His [1]coming;
>
> **B'** **9** *that is,* the one whose [1]coming is in accord with the activity of [a]Satan, with all power and [2b]signs and false wonders, **10** and with [1]all the deception of wickedness for [a]those who perish, because they did not receive the love of [b]the truth so as to be saved. **11** For this reason [a]God [1]will send upon them [2]a [b]deluding influence so that they will believe [3]what is false, **12** in order that they all may be [1]judged who [a]did not believe the truth, but [2b]took pleasure in wickedness.

A'   [a]But we should always give thanks to God for you, [b]brethren beloved by the Lord, because [c]God has chosen you [1]from the beginning [d]for salvation [2e]through sanctification [3]by the Spirit and faith in the truth. **14** It was for this He [a]called you through [b]our gospel, [1]that you may gain the glory of our Lord Jesus Christ. **15** So then, brethren, [a]stand firm and [b]hold to the traditions which you were taught, whether [c]by word *of mouth* or [d]by letter [1]from us. **16** [a]Now may our Lord Jesus Christ [a]Himself and God our Father, who has [b]loved us and given us eternal comfort and [c]good hope by grace, **17** [a]comfort and [b]strengthen your hearts in every good work and word.

Discussion

This chapter comprises one chiasm. It describes the "man of lawlessness."

Questioning the Passage

1. What "spirit" is going to alarm the people? (v. 2)

    It is an unidentified spirit that is going to alarm the people. It is not the Holy Spirit because the word "holy" is missing from the Greek and the Peshitta version (in the Greek version, the word for spirit would be capitalized). The spirit could refer to any person who appears before the congregation preaching that the end is near. Gnostics and other Christian expressions were a concern for Paul's Mithras converted House churches. He placed several warnings of this nature in most of his writings.

2. Why does Paul say the message from the spirit in verse two is not from him?

    As noted in the answer to question #1 of this section, Paul was concerned that "false" teachers would come to the congregation and claim that Paul sent them. Therefore, Paul must have sent something with his students to identify them as being with him.

3. Who or what is the "man of lawlessness," the son of perdition? (v. 3)

    "It appears more probable from the context that a general abandonment of the basis of civil order is envisaged. This is not only rebellion against the law of Moses; it is a large-scale revolt against public order, and since public order is maintained by the "governing authorities" who "have been instituted by God," any assault on it is an assault on a divine ordinance (Rom 13:1, 2). It is, in fact, the whole concept of divine authority over the world that is set at defiance in *"the* rebellion" par excellence."[5]

Paul saw anyone who preached any expression of Christianity except him as a messenger from Satan. If the Gnostic church survived, it would say the same thing about the proto-orthodox (Paul's) churches.

4. Is this chapter a warning to avoid any Christian expression except the one that Paul left them? (v. 1-4)

The theme of verses one through four can be seen in all of Paul's letters. Paul was possibly concerned that the Mithras house churches he converted still practiced the cult's rituals and beliefs. He worried the Gnostic Christians would reveal it as a rebranded pagan religion.

5. What is the mystery of lawlessness? (v. 7)

The mystery is something that was concealed and now shown to the people. Usually, it has something to do with the fulfillment of the LORD's ways. However, it is not identified in this letter.

"The "mystery of lawlessness" (formally antithetic to the τῆς εὐσεβείας μυστήριον, "the mystery of our religion," 1 Tim 3:16) is a satanic counterpart to the mystery of God's purpose; at present it works beneath the surface but when the due time comes for its disclosure it will find its embodiment in the manifested "man of lawlessness." Until then it is under restraint; μόνον ὁ κατέχων ἄρτι—but this time

---

[5] Bruce, F. F. (1982). *1 and 2 Thessalonians* (Vol. 45, p. 167). Word, Incorporated.

the restraining agency is personal (ὁ κατέχων, masculine, as against τὸ κατέχον, neuter, in v 6). The restrainer holds the mystery of lawlessness in check "until he is removed," ἕως ἐκ μέσου γένηται. The phrase ἐκ μέσου (without further qualification of the μέσον) in itself implies removal. For other instances of ἐκ μέσου γενέσθαι in Greek literature cf. Plutarch, *Timoleon* 5.3, "he decided to live by himself, having moved away (ἐκ μέσου γενόμενος) out of public view"; Achilles Tatius, *Leucippe and Clitophon* 2.27, "when Clio has been removed (τῆς Κλειοῦς ἐκ μέσου γενομένς)"; Ps.-Aeschines, Ep 12.6, "what they formerly covered up is clearly revealed, now that they have been removed (ἐκ μέσου γενομένων)"—i.e. by death or exile."[6]

6. Who is restraining the man of lawlessness? (v. 7)

"Anyone undertaking to identify the restraining agency must reckon with the fact that it may be viewed either personally (ὁ κατέχων) or impersonally (τὸ κατέχον). It is plain, moreover, that both the mystery of iniquity and the restraining agency are at work at the time of the writing of the epistle; the restrainer has not yet been removed, therefore the man of lawlessness has not yet appeared, and *a fortiori* the Day of the Lord has not yet arrived."[7]

7. Who is the man of lawlessness? (v. 8)

This man is called the Anti-Christ. He would perform miracles and lead numerous people away from Yeshua's teachings and especially away from Paul's teachings.

---

[6] Bruce, F. F. (1982). *1 and 2 Thessalonians* (Vol. 45, p. 170). Word, Incorporated.

[7] IBID.

8. How will Yeshua consume the man of lawlessness? (v. 8)

   Paul does not identify how this will be done. There is the general belief that good will always triumph over evil. Since Yeshua is good, he has to be triumphant.

9. What are the powers, signs and lying wonders? (v. 9)

   "ἐν πάσῃ δυνάμει καὶ σημείοις καὶ τέρασιν ψεύδους, "with all power and lying signs and wonders" (or "wonders of falsehood"; the adjectival genitive may qualify τέρασιν only, or (as is probable) σηνείοις καὶ τέρασιν, "lying signs and wonders," or even all three datives). The three substantives are used of the works of Jesus, e.g. in Acts 2:22, where Peter speaks of him as divinely attested by the δυνάμεις and τέρατα and σημεῖα "which God did through him"; similar works, attending the proclamation of the gospel, bore witness to the authority of the risen Christ by his Spirit in the message and its preachers (as in Acts 2:43; Gal 3:5; Heb 2:4). Here again the ministry of Jesus is parodied (cf. the σημεῖα μεγάλα of Rev 13:13, by which the earth-dwellers are persuaded to worship the imperial beast). Indeed, Jesus himself foretold that false Messiahs and false prophets would appear in the interval preceding the coming of the Son of Man "and show signs and wonders (σημεῖα καὶ τέρατα), to lead astray (ἀποπλανᾶν), if possible, the elect" (Mark 13:22 par. Matt 24:24)."[8]

10. Why would the LORD purposely deceive people? (v. 11)

    The LORD does not send evil into the world. However, the LORD does not stop people from allowing themselves to be consumed by evil. The warning is to seek proper spiritual counsel and good guidance. The evil people, especially the Anti-Christ, had rejected the truths of love and peace.

---

[8] Bruce, F. F. (1982). *1 and 2 Thessalonians* (Vol. 45, p. 173). Word, Incorporated.

11. How does Paul explain predestination? (v. 13)

To view this as predestination means that the LORD knew who was going to become followers of Yeshua. Then, by joining the movement, they will enter Heaven. The idea of being pre-chosen is not explained in the Pauline letters. It is later on that the church has to develop an answer to the question. The church answer is that when all souls were created, the LORD separated them, designating some to return to Heaven and for some not. Predestination as a doctrine is flawed because a person will never know if they are predestined to Heaven or Hell.

Culture Section

Discussion

The forging of letters and documents in the Near East is an old practice. Semitic letters, written in Aramaic, Hebrew and even Arabic, can be forged and changed by adding or eliminating a dot over a letter. The entire sentence would change meaning. Paul cautioned the Thessalonians about false prophets who wrongly foretold the sudden return of Yeshua, which would lead to the end of the world. Converts to Christianity were told that the earth's end was soon because Yeshua was about to return. When the rumor of Yeshua's return spread, it was difficult to change people's minds.

Numerical codes, symbols, or metaphors were used to criticize rulers or religious figures during Paul's time. For example, in the Revelation, the author referred to Nero Ceasar as the beast with the number six hundred sixty-six (666) on his head. This allowed people to write something against the authorities without being directly implicated.

Thoughts

The question about false prophets and false messengers of the Gospel is a problem that still exists today. The 1980s had many TV evangelists saying that if you sent them money, they would heal or bless people. Many of them were proven to be frauds. However, they were never forced to give back the money. Most of the time, the funds simply "disappeared." There are false prophets today who try to get congregations to fund their efforts. This would include organizations that say they are doing "Christian" deeds but are lining their pockets more than helping people. For example, Good Will was making money for its creator. Indeed, there are people who Good Will helps. However, it is not as charitable an organization as most people think it is.

Chapter Three

Language

Peshitta	New American Standard 1995
2Thessalonians 3:1 Henceforth, brethren, pray ye for us, that the word of our Lord may, in every place, run and be glorified, as with you; **2** and that we may be delivered from evil and perverse men; for faith is not in all. **3** And faithful is the Lord, who will keep you and rescue you from the evil One. **4** And we have confidence in you, through our Lord, that what we have inculcated on you, ye both have done, and will do. **5** And may our Lord direct your hearts to the love of God, and to a patient waiting for the Messiah. **6** And we enjoin upon you, my brethren, in the name of our Lord Jesus the Messiah, that ye withdraw from every brother who walketh wickedly, and not according to the precepts which ye received from us. **7** For ye know how ye ought to imitate us, who did not walk wickedly among you. **8** Neither did we eat bread gratuitously from any of you; but, with toil and weariness, we labored by night and by day, that we might not be burdensome to any of you. **9** It was not because we have no authority, but that we might give you an example in ourselves, that ye might imitate us. **10** And while we were with you, we also gave you this precept, That every one who would not work, should likewise not eat. **11** For we hear, there are some among you who walk wickedly, and do nothing except vain things. **12** Now such persons, we command and exhort, by our Lord Jesus	**2Thessalonians 3:1** [a]Finally, brethren, [b]pray for us that [c]the word of the Lord will [1]spread rapidly and be glorified, just as *it did* also with you; **2** and that we will be [a]rescued from [1]perverse and evil men; for not all have [2]faith. **3** But [a]the Lord is faithful, [1]and He will strengthen and protect you [2]from [b]the evil *one*. **4** We have [a]confidence in the Lord concerning you, that you [b]are doing and will *continue to* do what we command. **5** May the Lord [a]direct your hearts into the love of God and into the steadfastness of Christ.

2Thessalonians 3:6 Now we command you, brethren, [a]in the name of our Lord Jesus Christ, that you [1b]keep away from every brother who [2]leads an [3c]unruly life and not according to [d]the tradition which [4]you received from us. **7** For you yourselves know how you ought to [1a]follow our example, because we did not act in an undisciplined manner among you, **8** nor did we [a]eat [1]anyone's bread [2]without paying for it, but with [b]labor and hardship we *kept* [c]working night and day so that we would not be a burden to any of you; **9** not because we do not have [a]the right *to this,* but in order to offer ourselves [b]as a model for you, so that you would [1]follow our example. **10** For even [a]when we were with you, we used to give you this order: [b]if anyone is not willing to work, then he is not to eat, either. **11** For |

the Messiah, that in quietness they work, and eat their own bread. **13** And my brethren, let it not be wearisome to you, to do what is good. **14** And if any one hearkeneth not to these [my] words in this epistle, separate that man from you, and have no intimacy with him, that he may be ashamed. **15** Yet, hold him not as an enemy, but admonish him as a brother. **16** And may the Lord of peace give you peace, always, in every thing. Our Lord be with you all. **17** The salutation in the writing of my own hand, I Paul have written it; which is the token in all my epistles, so I write. **18** The grace of Jesus the Messiah be with you all, my brethren. Amen.

we hear that some among you are [a]leading an undisciplined life, doing no work at all, but acting like [b]busybodies. **12** Now such persons we command and [a]exhort in the Lord Jesus Christ to [b]work in quiet fashion and eat their own bread. **13** But as for you, [a]brethren, [b]do not grow weary of doing good.

2Thessalonians 3:14 If anyone does not obey our [1]instruction [2a]in this letter, take special note of that person [3b]and do not associate with him, so that he will be [c]put to shame. **15** *Yet* [a]do not regard him as an enemy, but [1b]admonish him as a [c]brother.

2Thessalonians 3:16 Now [a]may the Lord of peace [b]Himself continually grant you peace in every [1]circumstance. [c]The Lord be with you all!

2Thessalonians 3:17 [1]I, Paul, write this greeting [a]with my own hand, and this is a distinguishing mark in every letter; this is the way I write. **18** [a]The grace of our Lord Jesus Christ be with you all.

References to the New American Standard 1995

2Thessalonians 3:1

[1]Lit *run*
[a]1 Thess 4:1
[b]1 Thess 5:25
[c]1 Thess 1:8

2Thessalonians 3:2

[1]Lit *improper*
[2]Or *the faith*
[a]Rom 15:31

2Thessalonians 3:3

[1]Lit *who will*
[2]Or *from evil*
[a]1 Cor 1:9; 1 Thess 5:24
[b]Matt 5:37

2Thessalonians 3:4

[a]2 Cor 2:3
[b]1 Thess 4:10

2Thessalonians 3:5

[a]1 Thess 3:11

2Thessalonians 3:6

[1]Or *avoid*
[2]Lit *walks disorderly*
[3]Or *undisciplined*
[4]One early ms reads *they*
[a]1 Cor 5:4
[b]Rom 16:17; 1 Cor 5:11; 2 Thess 3:14
[c]1 Thess 5:14; 2 Thess 3:7, 11
[d]1 Cor 11:2; 2 Thess 2:15

2Thessalonians 3:7

[1]Lit *imitate us*
[a]1 Thess 1:6; 2 Thess 3:9

2Thessalonians 3:8
[1]Lit *from anyone*
[2]Lit *freely*
[a]1 Cor 9:4
[b]1 Thess 2:9
[c]Acts 18:3; Eph 4:28

2Thessalonians 3:9
[1]Lit *imitate us*
[a]1 Cor 9:4ff
[b]2 Thess 3:7

2Thessalonians 3:10
[a]1 Thess 3:4
[b]1 Thess 4:11

2Thessalonians 3:11
[a]2 Thess 3:6
[b]1 Tim 5:13; 1 Pet 4:15

2Thessalonians 3:12
[a]1 Thess 4:1
[b]1 Thess 4:11

2Thessalonians 3:13
[a]1 Thess 4:1
[b]2 Cor 4:1; Gal 6:9

2Thessalonians 3:14
[1]Lit *word*
[2]Lit *through*
[3]Lit *not to associate*
[a]Col 4:16
[b]2 Thess 3:6
[c]1 Cor 4:14

2Thessalonians 3:15
[1]Or *keep admonishing*
[a]Gal 6:1
[b]1 Thess 5:14

*c*2 Thess 3:6, 13

2Thessalonians 3:16
[1]Lit *way*
*a*Rom 15:33
*b*1 Thess 3:11
*c*Ruth 2:4

2Thessalonians 3:17
[1]Lit *The greeting by my hand of Paul*
*a*1 Cor 16:21

2Thessalonians 3:18

Koine Greek

2Thessalonians 3:1 Τὸ λοιπόν, προσεύχεσθε, ἀδελφοί, περὶ ἡμῶν, ἵνα ὁ λόγος τοῦ κυρίου τρέχῃ καὶ δοξάζηται, καθὼς καὶ πρὸς ὑμᾶς, **2** καὶ ἵνα ῥυσθῶμεν ἀπὸ τῶν ἀτόπων καὶ πονηρῶν ἀνθρώπων· οὐ γὰρ πάντων ἡ πίστις. **3** Πιστὸς δέ ἐστιν ὁ κύριος, ὃς στηρίξει ὑμᾶς καὶ φυλάξει ἀπὸ τοῦ πονηροῦ. **4** Πεποίθαμεν δὲ ἐν κυρίῳ ἐφ᾽ ὑμᾶς, ὅτι ἃ παραγγέλλομεν ὑμῖν, καὶ ποιεῖτε καὶ ποιήσετε. **5** Ὁ δὲ κύριος κατευθύναι ὑμῶν τὰς καρδίας εἰς τὴν ἀγάπην τοῦ θεοῦ, καὶ εἰς τὴν ὑπομονὴν τοῦ χριστοῦ.

2Thessalonians 3:6 Παραγγέλλομεν δὲ ὑμῖν, ἀδελφοί, ἐν ὀνόματι τοῦ κυρίου ἡμῶν Ἰησοῦ χριστοῦ, στέλλεσθαι ὑμᾶς ἀπὸ παντὸς ἀδελφοῦ ἀτάκτως περιπατοῦντος, καὶ μὴ κατὰ τὴν παράδοσιν ἣν παρέλαβον παρ᾽ ἡμῶν. **7** Αὐτοὶ γὰρ οἴδατε πῶς δεῖ μιμεῖσθαι ἡμᾶς· ὅτι οὐκ ἠτακτήσαμεν ἐν ὑμῖν, **8** οὐδὲ δωρεὰν ἄρτον ἐφάγομεν παρά τινος, ἀλλ᾽ ἐν κόπῳ καὶ μόχθῳ, νύκτα καὶ ἡμέραν ἐργαζόμενοι, πρὸς τὸ μὴ ἐπιβαρῆσαί τινα ὑμῶν· **9** οὐχ ὅτι οὐκ ἔχομεν ἐξουσίαν, ἀλλ᾽ ἵνα ἑαυτοὺς τύπον δῶμεν ὑμῖν εἰς τὸ μιμεῖσθαι ἡμᾶς. **10** Καὶ γὰρ ὅτε ἦμεν πρὸς ὑμᾶς, τοῦτο παρηγγέλλομεν ὑμῖν ὅτι εἴ τις οὐ θέλει ἐργάζεσθαι, μηδὲ ἐσθιέτω. **11** Ἀκούομεν γὰρ τινας περιπατοῦντας ἐν ὑμῖν ἀτάκτως, μηδὲν ἐργαζομένους, ἀλλὰ περιεργαζομένους. **12** Τοῖς δὲ τοιούτοις παραγγέλλομεν καὶ παρακαλοῦμεν διὰ τοῦ κυρίου ἡμῶν Ἰησοῦ χριστοῦ, ἵνα μετὰ ἡσυχίας ἐργαζόμενοι τὸν ἑαυτῶν ἄρτον ἐσθίωσιν. **13** Ὑμεῖς δέ, ἀδελφοί, μὴ ἐκκακήσητε καλοποιοῦντες. **14** Εἰ δέ τις οὐχ ὑπακούει τῷ λόγῳ ἡμῶν διὰ τῆς ἐπιστολῆς, τοῦτον σημειοῦσθε, καὶ μὴ συναναμίγνυσθε αὐτῷ, ἵνα ἐντραπῇ, **15** καὶ μὴ ὡς ἐχθρὸν ἡγεῖσθε, ἀλλὰ νουθετεῖτε ὡς ἀδελφόν.

2Thessalonians 3:16 Αὐτὸς δὲ ὁ κύριος τῆς εἰρήνης δῴη ὑμῖν τὴν εἰρήνην διὰ παντὸς ἐν παντὶ τρόπῳ. Ὁ κύριος μετὰ πάντων ὑμῶν.

2Thessalonians 3:17 Ὁ ἀσπασμὸς τῇ ἐμῇ χειρὶ Παύλου, ὅ ἐστιν σημεῖον ἐν πάσῃ ἐπιστολῇ· οὕτως γράφω. **18** Ἡ χάρις τοῦ κυρίου ἡμῶν Ἰησοῦ χριστοῦ μετὰ πάντων ὑμῶν. Ἀμήν.

Language

  Process of Discovery

   Linguistics Section

    Linguistic Structure

[Prayer request] 2Thessalonians 3:1 [a]Finally, brethren, [b]pray for us that [c]the word of the Lord will [1]spread rapidly and be glorified, just as *it did* also with you; **2** and that we will be [a]rescued from [1]perverse and evil men; for not all have [2]faith. **3** But [a]the Lord is faithful, [1]and He will strengthen and protect you [2]from [b]the evil *one*. **4** We have [a]confidence in the Lord concerning you, that you [b]are doing and will *continue to* do what we command. **5** May the Lord [a]direct your hearts into the love of God and into the steadfastness of Christ.

[Commandment] 2Thessalonians 3:6 Now we command you, brethren, [a]in the name of our Lord Jesus Christ, that you [1b]keep away from every brother who [2]leads an [3c]unruly life and not according to [d]the tradition which [4]you received from us. **7** For you yourselves know how you ought to [1a]follow our example, because we did not act in an undisciplined manner among you, **8** nor did we [a]eat [1]anyone's bread [2]without paying for it, but with [b]labor and hardship we *kept* [c]working night and day so that we would not be a burden to any of you; **9** not because we do not have [a]the right *to this,* but in order to offer ourselves [b]as a model for you, so that you would [1]follow our example. **10** For even [a]when we were with you, we used to give you this order: [b]if anyone is not willing to work, then he is not to eat, either. **11** For we hear that some among you are [a]leading an undisciplined life, doing no work at all, but acting like [b]busybodies. **12** Now such persons we command and [a]exhort in the Lord Jesus Christ to [b]work in quiet fashion and eat their own bread. **13** But as for you, [a]brethren, [b]do not grow weary of doing good.

[Excommunication] 2Thessalonians 3:14 If anyone does not obey our [1]instruction [2a]in this letter, take special note of that person [3b]and do not associate with him, so that he will be [c]put to shame. **15** *Yet* [a]do not regard him as an enemy, but [1b]admonish him as a [c]brother.

[Final blessing] 2Thessalonians 3:16 Now [a]may the Lord of peace [b]Himself continually grant you peace in every [1]circumstance. [c]The Lord be with you all!

[Closing] 2Thessalonians 3:17 [1]I, Paul, write this greeting [a]with my own hand, and this is a distinguishing mark in every letter; this is the way I write. **18** [a]The grace of our Lord Jesus Christ be with you all.

Discussion

The third chapter is a prayer request followed by instructions. It is difficult to understand that Paul opposed Yeshua's words when he said do not associate with anyone who does not follow his instructions. Paul is specifically referring to Gnostic Christians and any other expression of Christianity that was not from him. Paul decided he knew everything that needed to be known about Yeshua's life. It is debatable that Paul knew everything. There were a lot of questions and definitions that Yeshua did not supply us. There is a potent mix of Mithras doctrine and rituals in the instructions Paul gives.

Questioning the Passage

1. What does it mean for the word of the Lord to be glorified? (v. 1)

   This instruction is that the members of the community must follow the ways of Yeshua. When a person follows Yeshua's words and actions, it glorifies Yeshua. The world thus sees Yeshua because the person is emulating him.

2. What does it mean for the Lord to be faithful? (v. 2)

   This is connected to glorifying the LORD. To be faithful to Yeshua means to follow his words and actions. When a church person is kind when in church but is nasty when outside of church, they are not faithful to Yeshua. Being faithful to Yeshua is a full-time job. Every situation and person must be dealt with in the same manner that Yeshua would have dealt with them

3. How does the Lord strengthen and protect? (v. 3)

    "In this verse Paul and his coworkers express their confidence in the Lord. Because God is faithful, He could be trusted to strengthen the Thessalonians and protect them from Satan. Because God is faithful He will not allow evil men to gain a victory over believers.

    The Bible assures us that God is completely trustworthy. Even when circumstances seem dim, He is faithful to sustain His people and bring good out of bad (Romans 8:28–29). Even when the prophet Jeremiah grieved over the fall of Jerusalem, he took courage in knowing that God is faithful. He wrote in Lamentations 3:21–23, "But this I call to mind, and therefore I have hope: The steadfast love of the LORD never ceases; his mercies never come to an end; they are new every morning; great is your faithfulness." The Lord is faithful to provide for our daily needs (Matthew 6:33; Philippians 4:19), and to provide the way of escape when we are tempted and tried (1 Corinthians 10:13)."[9]

4. "The evil one" is it a commentator comment? (v. 3)

    The "evil one" is a reference to Satan. It would have been applied to people who came to the congregation and told them that Paul did not instruct them properly about Christianity. It is not written in the verse but heavily implied.

5. What does confidence in the Lord mean? (v. 4)

    Confidence in the Lord means one has hope, faith and trust in what Yeshua said he would do for humanity.

---

[9] 1. "2 Thessalonians 3:3," BibleRef.com, accessed October 3, 2023, https://www.bibleref.com/2-Thessalonians/3/2-Thessalonians-3-3.html.

6. Why does Paul feel to command the people to follow his ways? (v. 4)

   Paul was extremely egocentric. He believed he had the only way to serve the LORD and to understand Yeshua the Messiah. When he converted Mithras House Churches, there was very little he changed. He did not have copies of Scripture nor a book of discipline (like the Didache [Christian behavior manual written around 150 CE]) to leave them. Paul adopted most, if not all, of the Mithras culture and rituals. The triune Mithras god of the Father, Mithras, Spirit became, the Father, Yeshua, and Spirit.

7. What does verse five mean?

   Paul was telling the members of the congregation that the LORD (God) would direct their hearts into a full discipleship to Yeshua as the Messiah. For the Mithras churches, the understanding of the Messiah as the second person of their god head definition worked. For Jewish communities, they did not expect the Messiah to be divine, but would have more power and abilities than a regular prophet. The Messiah was to be followed because he instructed the people to live in a godly manner.

8. What does "in the name of our Lord Jesus Christ" mean (v. 6)

   The church completely misunderstood this phrase today. This is because Christianity moved from being a Near East religion to becoming a Greek-based religion. This phrase is a Semitic idiom which means "As a student of Jesus Christ I do the same."

9. Why is it wrong to be idle? (v. 6)

    Idleness can allow Evil Inclination to enter one's heart and thus become attached to Satan. Also, in the original communities, every person had a task to perform. The early Christian communities were small. The Mithras House Churches were usually under 50 (sometimes a lot fewer) people. When they formed into a commune, it was necessary for all members to pull their weight. When the Roman persecutions started, the commune became a place to find refuge.

10. Why do we need to keep away from people who are idle? (v. 6)

    This can be viewed as a general statement about being around evil people. If you hang out with people who are idle, you may become idle too. After all, you see that doing nothing works. Again, being small communities, there was no room for idle people. Everyone needed to perform come task.

11. Why was it important for people to work? (v. 10)

    The answer to this question can be found in the answers to questions nine and ten.

12. Why is being a busybody a bad thing? (v. 11)

    A busybody is also called a gossiper. Gossip destroys communities because the truth gets deformed as the story makes its way throughout the community. If you ever played "telephone" as a child, you would remember how the message from the first person in the chain was changed when it got to the last person. Gossip, especially when false, will destroy a community or congregation. This can be seen in churches today.

13. What does "exhort in the Lord Jesus Christ" mean? (v. 12)

Paul uses this phrase to imply that Yeshua told him to make the exhortation. Therefore, the people must follow Paul's orders because they are indirectly from Yeshua.

14. Is Paul saying excommunicate a person in verse fourteen?

The simple answer is "yes." Paul was so scared about the other expressions of Christianity in the Roman World that he told his churches that they were not allowed to talk to members of these other expressions. Today, this can be seen when the Catholic church tells its members that they will go to Hell if they take communion in a Protestant church.

15. Why did it mean to be ashamed? (v. 14)

To be ashamed means to be embarrassed by one's words or actions. Paul did not like people from other Christian expressions in his congregations.

Thoughts

Without the questions that Paul is responding to, it is difficult to understand the purpose of this chapter and, in fact, the entire letter. The bottom line for Paul is that this congregation must learn to spot people from outside Christian expressions and not allow them to enter the congregation. If one gets in, it is the responsibility of the community to excommunicate that person. There were a lot of challenges to Paul's conversion of Mithras House Churches from the Gnostic Christians of Northern Egypt and the Jewish believers in Yeshua as Messiah from Jerusalem and other places in the Empire.

Bibliography

Introduction to the Methodology

"Erasmus Greek New Testament." Insight of the King. Accessed October 3, 2023. https://www.insightoftheking.com/erasmus-greek-new-testament.html.

Errico, Rocco A., and George M. Lamsa. *Aramaic light on Galatians through hebrews: A commentary based on Aramaic, the language of jesus, and ancient near eastern customs.* Smyma, GA: Noohra Foundation, 2005.

"A List of the 613 Mitzvot (Commandments)." A List of the 613 Mitzvot (Commandments) - Judaism 101 (JewFAQ). Accessed October 3, 2023. https://www.jewfaq.org/613_commandments.

From the Chapters

"2 Thessalonians 3:3." BibleRef.com. Accessed October 3, 2023. https://www.bibleref.com/2-Thessalonians/3/2-Thessalonians-3-3.html.

"2 Thessalonians 3:3." BibleRef.com. Accessed October 3, 2023. https://www.bibleref.com/2-Thessalonians/3/2-Thessalonians-3-3.html.

Bing. Accessed September 10, 2023. https://www.bing.com/images.

Bruce, F. F. *1 and 2 thessalonians.* Grand Rapids, MI: Zondervan, 2015.